ADHD STRATEGIES FOR SUCCESS

Empowering Strategies For Dealing With Adult ADHD

JOSE D. PAXTON

Table Of Content

Introduction

Welcome to "Success Strategies for ADHD," a book particularly created to help you handle the hurdles and release the great potential that lies inside you. If you are reading this, chances are you or someone close to you is battling with Attention Deficit Hyperactivity Disorder (ADHD), and you want direction on how to overcome its difficulties and prosper in all facets of life.

Imagine a future where ADHD is not perceived as a hindrance but as a distinct ability. This book strives to empower people with ADHD by giving practical solutions, useful insights, and a supportive framework for attaining success and satisfaction. Through a mix of research-backed approaches, personal experiences, and the tales of those who have won over ADHD, we will begin on a transforming journey together.

Before we get into the methods and tools, let me offer a personal tale that could relate to your own experiences. Picture a young pupil sitting in a classroom, attempting to keep focused on the teacher's lesson. Thoughts and ideas rush into their head, a tornado of inventiveness and curiosity, making it tough to focus on the work at hand. The student's restlessness and impulsivity frequently led to missed deadlines and unsatisfactory performance, leaving them feeling disappointed and inadequate. Does this sound familiar?

That student was me.

Growing up with ADHD was tough, but it also cleared the path for self-discovery and the development of unique skills. It was through trial and error, and with the help of a loving family and understanding mentors, that I learned to accept my ADHD and navigate the world with purpose and perseverance. This path inspired a desire inside me to assist individuals with ADHD attain their full potential and overcome the difficulties they confront.

"Success Strategies for ADHD" is designed with you in mind - whether you are a student battling with scholastic obligations, a professional aiming to achieve in your field, or someone just seeking a satisfying and balanced life. Together, we will study a broad variety of issues, from understanding the subtleties of ADHD to practical approaches for time management, organization, attention, and more. We will dig into emotional well-being, creating healthy habits, and fostering meaningful relationships.

But this book goes beyond techniques and ideas. It is a testimonial to the amazing skills and talents that people with ADHD possess. Neurodiversity is not a problem to be remedied, but a magnificent part of human variety that gives new insights and imaginative thinking. We will celebrate the strength of creativity, resilience, and drive that resides inside you, enabling you to succeed in a world that may not always understand your neurobiology.

As we start on this journey together, I ask you to open your mind and heart to the possibilities that lie ahead. Each chapter will empower you with practical skills, insights, and inspiration to handle the hurdles of ADHD and discover your real potential. Remember, success is not defined by conformance to conventional conventions, but by the progress you accomplish on your terms.

Now is the moment to embrace your ADHD, use its qualities, and begin on a road toward success, satisfaction, and self-acceptance. Let's begin on this transforming adventure together and redefine what it means to achieve with ADHD.

Welcome to "Success Strategies for ADHD."

Chapter 1:Understanding ADHD: An Overview of Attention Deficit Hyperactivity Disorder

When you think of Attention Deficit Hyperactivity Disorder (ADHD), you may have a rudimentary idea of its symptoms, but let's go further into its nuances. ADHD is a neurodevelopmental disease that affects people of all ages, characterized by persistent patterns of inattention, hyperactivity, and impulsivity. The symptoms present differently in each individual, but they profoundly impair numerous parts of life.

For many people with ADHD, inattention is a considerable difficulty. You can find it difficult to retain attention on chores or discussions, leading to frequent blunders or missing facts. Simple things like organizing your stuff or completing homework might seem onerous and easily fall through the gaps. This difficulty with focus might leave you feeling dissatisfied, nervous, and questioning your ability.

Hyperactivity and impulsivity, the other features of ADHD, may appear in restlessness, fidgeting, and a continual desire for movement. You could have encountered difficulties sitting still during meetings or lectures, which can be mistaken as a lack of attention or participation. Impulsivity may cause you to act without contemplating the implications, sometimes resulting in fast choices or impulsive acts that you later regret.

Debunking Common Misconceptions Regarding ADHD

ADHD is a disorder that is frequently surrounded by myths and prejudices. It is crucial to refute these assumptions to promote a better knowledge of the illness. Contrary to common assumptions, ADHD is not just a consequence of laziness or a lack of discipline. It is a neurobiological illness based on the intricate interaction of genetic, environmental, and neurological variables.

Another widespread misperception is that ADHD exclusively affects children. While symptoms often develop throughout infancy, ADHD may continue into adolescence and maturity. In reality, many people obtain a diagnosis in maturity, discovering that their troubles were due to undiagnosed ADHD.

It's also vital to debunk the misconception that ADHD is merely an excuse or a diagnosis. ADHD is a real medical illness recognized by major health organizations worldwide. By understanding the physiological foundation of ADHD, you may reframe your viewpoint and build empathy for yourself or others who encounter the obstacles it poses.

The Impact of ADHD on Personal and Professional Life

ADHD has a dramatic influence on both personal and professional domains, frequently extending beyond the acute symptoms. In personal relationships, the issues associated with ADHD may strain communication and emotional bonds. The inattentiveness, impulsivity, and disorganization may inadvertently generate misconceptions, leading to irritation and disputes with loved ones.

Professionally, ADHD might bring distinct problems. Tasks that demand continuous attention or thorough planning may be more tough, resulting in missed deadlines or completed projects. However, it is vital to realize that ADHD does not determine your talents or potential for success. With the correct tactics and support, people with ADHD have exhibited extraordinary success in a broad variety of professions.

Understanding the symptoms, refuting misunderstandings, and acknowledging the effect of ADHD are key steps for managing the intricacies of the illness. By acquiring broad knowledge, you may begin to design methods and techniques that maximize your strengths while tackling the obstacles ADHD provides. In the next chapters, we will examine a plethora of success methods to help you grow and unleash your full potential, accepting ADHD as a component of your unique path toward success and satisfaction.

Chapter 2: The Power of Self-Awareness: Embracing Your ADHD

As I think about my personal experience, I distinctly remember the key moment when I got my ADHD diagnosis. Initially, it was welcomed with a tornado of feelings — a combination of relief, perplexity, and even a sense of loss. However, identifying and embracing my diagnosis represented the first step towards self-awareness and personal progress.

Recognizing your ADHD diagnosis is not an admission of weakness or failure; it is a recognition of your unique neurology. It is a chance to obtain a greater awareness of yourself, your abilities, and the areas where you may experience obstacles. By embracing your diagnosis, you open the door to self-discovery, compassion, and the potential of establishing a meaningful life.

Understanding Your Strengths and Weaknesses

Understanding your talents and shortcomings is a fundamental component of self-awareness. ADHD may offer some obstacles, but it also carries with it a range of qualities and abilities. By identifying and using these qualities, you may navigate the world with confidence and resilience.

For instance, people with ADHD typically show extraordinary creativity and out-of-the-box thinking. Our brains have an exceptional capacity to create unique connections and to perceive possibilities where others may not. This creativity may be focused towards creative activities, problem-solving, or business initiatives, enabling us to make a major influence in our chosen industries.

On the other hand, it is necessary to admit our flaws and areas where we may suffer. Organization, time management, and continuous attention may create obstacles. However, by knowing these vulnerabilities, we may build solutions and seek help to lessen their influence on our everyday life.

Developing a Positive Mindset towards Your Condition

Developing a positive perspective toward your ADHD is a revolutionary step on your road toward success and self-acceptance. It requires reframing your viewpoint, appreciating your neurodiversity, and accepting that ADHD is not a restriction but a distinct component of your personality.

Consider the example of Emma, a successful businesswoman who found her ADHD later in life. Initially, she considered her diagnosis as a setback, worrying that it might limit her career objectives. However, as she went on a path of self-discovery, she found that her ADHD drove her creativity, intuition, and capacity to think beyond the box. With her newfound positive perspective, Emma developed a profitable company that valued her particular abilities and had a meaningful effect.

Embracing your ADHD is not about disregarding the issues it provides; rather, it is about finding methods, getting assistance, and embracing self-compassion. It's about acknowledging that you are not defined by your diagnosis but by your resilience, drive, and ability to progress.

By adopting a positive mentality, you empower yourself to manage the ups and downs of life with confidence and grace. You learn to enjoy the road, accepting both the accomplishments and the disappointments as chances for development and self-improvement.

In the chapters that follow, we will go further into practical tactics and strategies that harness the potential of self-awareness. By acknowledging and embracing your ADHD diagnosis, knowing your particular talents and limitations, and creating a positive mentality, you will begin on a revolutionary journey toward success and self-fulfillment.

Remember, you are not alone on this path. There is a lively community of people with ADHD who have flourished and achieved great achievement. Together, let us embrace our neurodiversity, release our potential, and reinvent what it means to live a meaningful life with ADHD.

Chapter 3: Building an Effective Support System

When I launched on my adventure with ADHD, I immediately learned the great benefit of having a solid support system around me. Family and friends play a critical role in understanding, embracing, and supporting those with ADHD. Their love, understanding, and tolerance may make a world of difference in managing the obstacles and appreciating the positives that come with ADHD.

In my personal experience, I recall how my parents played a vital role in my path. They took an effort to educate themselves about ADHD, attending seminars and seeking help from professionals. Their empathy and support made me feel acknowledged and inspired me to explore techniques and skills to manage my symptoms efficiently.

Friends may also play a key role in assisting those with ADHD. True friends understand and accept us for who we are, including our unique idiosyncrasies and struggles. They give a listening ear, encouragement, and practical help when required. Whether it's reminding you of critical deadlines or giving you a safe area for you to voice your emotions, friends may be a great source of support and understanding.

Seeking Professional Help: Therapists, Coaches, and Mentors

While the support of family and friends is crucial, obtaining professional aid may give extra insight and specialized experience. Therapists, coaches, and mentors may give a systematic framework to address the unique issues associated with ADHD.

Therapists knowledgeable in ADHD may help clients build coping methods, strengthen executive function abilities, and address any emotional issues that may emerge. Through counseling, I discovered efficient techniques to handle stress, boost my attention, and control my emotions. The assistance and resources I gained from my therapist were vital in my personal development and path toward achievement.

Coaches and mentors may also give personalized assistance and direction to people with ADHD. These specialists understand the particular problems and strengths associated with ADHD, giving techniques to enhance time management, organization, and goal-setting. For example, I worked with a coach who helped me establish systems and routines that matched my ADHD inclinations, helping me to excel in my academic and professional interests.

Joining Support Groups and Communities for ADHD

Connecting with individuals who have similar experiences is a great approach to creating support and feeling a sense of belonging. Joining support groups and networks for those with ADHD may give a safe area to share thoughts, trade solutions, and get encouragement from others who genuinely understand the issues we experience.

In my quest, I discovered peace and inspiration in an ADHD support group. Sharing our experiences, achievements, and disappointments with those who had traveled a similar route generated a feeling of kinship and understanding. We celebrated one other's achievements, gave encouragement through tough times, and discussed practical solutions that had proved beneficial for controlling ADHD symptoms.

Today, with the accessibility of online networks, it is simpler than ever to interact with like-minded folks globally. Online forums, social media groups, and virtual support networks enable us to reach out for assistance, exchange information, and find inspiration from varied views.

Building an effective support system entails maintaining connections with family and friends, getting help from specialists, and engaging with a community that understands the specific difficulties of ADHD. Together, they establish a network of support, encouragement, and understanding that encourages us to overcome difficulties, embrace our strengths, and live a full life with ADHD.

Chapter 4: Time Management and Organization Strategies

When it comes to controlling ADHD, having successful routines and timetables may be a game-changer. Developing a systematic framework helps bring order and consistency to your everyday life. Let's study some real-life instances to highlight the power of routines and timetables.

Imagine waking up each morning and following a consistent routine that sets the tone for the day ahead. You may start with a few minutes of mindfulness or exercise to calm your thoughts and enhance your energy. Then, having a specific time for breakfast, getting dressed, and arranging your possessions enables a seamless transition into the day.

Throughout the day, you may arrange distinct time blocks for various activities, such as work or study sessions, breaks for physical exercise or relaxation, and even specified time for hobbies or self-care. By developing a routine, you create a structure that helps enhance your productivity and manage your ADHD symptoms more efficiently.

Section 2: Prioritizing Tasks and Setting Realistic Goals

In the tornado of everyday duties and obligations, it's vital to focus and create reasonable objectives. ADHD may sometimes make it tough to concentrate on a single activity, resulting in a sensation of overload. However, by applying effective tactics, you may reclaim control and achieve what counts.

Start by breaking down significant activities into smaller, achievable stages. This strategy enables you to handle one component at a time, eliminating the impression of being overwhelmed. For example, if you have a research paper to finish, break it down into steps like researching, planning, writing drafts, and revising. Concentrating on one step at a time, you sustain momentum and generate a feeling of success.

To prioritize work properly, try utilizing the Eisenhower Matrix. This tool categorizes jobs based on their urgency and relevance, letting you understand what needs urgent attention and what can be assigned or postponed. By utilizing this strategy, you can better organize your time and energy, ensuring that you concentrate on high-priority projects that correspond with your objectives.

Utilizing Tools and Apps for Time Management and Organization

In the digital era, a vast selection of tools and applications are available to aid with time management and organizing. These technology solutions may be especially advantageous for those with ADHD. Let's study some instances.

Digital calendars and task management tools, such as Google Calendar, Todoist, or Trello, provide customized options to help you keep organized. You may build color-coded plans, set reminders, and make deadlines to ensure that you keep on track with your obligations.

For folks who thrive with visual assistance, things like whiteboards, sticky notes, or physical calendars may give a practical and adaptable approach to managing activities. For instance, you may design a visual board with distinct parts reflecting certain aspects of your life (e.g., professional, personal, health). Within each area, you may use sticky notes or write directly on the board to manage chores and objectives.

Remember, selecting the best tools and applications is a personal adventure. Experiment with numerous alternatives to find what works best for you and corresponds with your ADHD inclinations and preferences.

By applying good time management and organizing tactics, you can recover control of your everyday life and enhance your productivity. Whether it's forming routines, setting realistic objectives, or leveraging tools and apps, these tactics allow you to harness your ADHD strengths and manage your obstacles more successfully. With practice and persistence, you will establish a customized strategy that helps you to flourish and accomplish your objectives.

Chapter 5: Overcoming Procrastination and Enhancing Focus

Procrastination is a typical difficulty addressed by people with ADHD. Understanding the underlying reasons and recognizing triggers might help you build solutions to overcome this inclination. Let's investigate some real-life situations to explain how to overcome frequent reasons for procrastination.

One typical cause is the fear of failure or perfectionism. You can find yourself postponing a task because you worry about not achieving your high expectations. In such instances, it's crucial to readjust your perspective and remind yourself that progress is more important than perfection. Breaking things into smaller, achievable stages may help lessen the overwhelming strain and make it easier to get started.

Another cause is feeling overwhelmed by a task's intricacy or immensity. This might lead to a sensation of paralysis, forcing you to put off doing the work completely. By employing the "divide and conquer" technique, you may reduce the work into smaller, more manageable sections. Focus on one area at a time, gradually generating momentum and lowering the seeming complexity.

Strategies to Improve Focus and Concentration

Enhancing attention and concentration is crucial to controlling ADHD efficiently. Let's discuss ways that may assist increase your capacity to remain focused in various scenarios.

Creating an appropriate setting for concentrating is key. Minimize distractions by locating a quiet area, shutting off alerts on your phone or computer, and wearing noise-canceling headphones if required. You may also find it beneficial to experiment with other environmental signals, such as background music or ambient noise, to determine what enhances your attention.

Chunking and timeboxing are useful approaches for controlling attention and enhancing productivity. Chunking is splitting huge jobs into smaller, more manageable bits. By concentrating on one piece at a time, you can retain attention and make progress. Timeboxing, on the other hand, entails establishing exact time limitations for tasks or activities. By establishing defined periods to concentrate on certain projects, you generate a feeling of urgency and organization that helps enhance attention.

Utilizing Techniques such as the Pomodoro Technique and Time Blocking

The Pomodoro Technique and time blocking are famous practices that help boost attention and productivity. Let's investigate how they operate and present real-life instances.

The Pomodoro Technique involves splitting your work into scheduled periods, often 25 minutes of intense work followed by a brief rest. After completing a specified number of intervals, you take a longer lengthier break.

This strategy enables you to work in small bursts, retaining attention throughout the allotted times and allowing frequent rests to recover. For example, you may set a timer for 25 minutes and concentrate completely on writing a report, then take a 5-minute break to stretch or relax before beginning the next Pomodoro session.

Time blocking is a way of allocating allocated blocks of time for certain tasks or activities. It helps you dedicate concentrated time to critical tasks and minimizes distractions and disruptions. For instance, you may devote a certain time block each day for crucial business activities, during which you switch off alerts and focus completely on the chosen activity.

By adopting tactics such as recognizing triggers, boosting attention and concentration, and applying techniques like the Pomodoro Technique and time blocking, you may fight procrastination and increase your ability to remain focused. These tactics allow you to take charge of your time, manage distractions, and achieve increased productivity and success. Remember, it's a path of trial and error, so experiment with various tactics to discover what works best for you.

Chapter 6: Boosting Productivity: Strategies for Getting Things Done

Example: Tackling a Daunting Work Project
Imagine you have a big work assignment with several deliverables and deadlines. Instead of feeling overwhelmed, break it down into tiny, achievable stages.

Start by describing the project's components and assigning specified milestones. For instance, allocate one day to completing research, another for crafting an outline, and the following days for writing particular parts. By concentrating on one task at a time, you'll experience a feeling of accomplishment and success, making the endeavor more achievable.

Example: Organizing a Cluttered Space
Cleaning and cleaning a messy area may be overwhelming. To enhance productivity, break the job into smaller regions or groups. Start with

one part of the room or concentrate on decluttering certain objects like books or clothing. With each finished portion, you'll experience a feeling of satisfaction, inspiring you to tackle the next region until the whole room is arranged.

Example: Studying for Exams
When presented with a pile of study material, it's easy to feel overwhelmed. Instead, divide the material into short study sessions. Focus on learning one idea or chapter at a time, and frequently check your progress. By splitting the content into digestible bits, you'll absorb the knowledge more efficiently and keep motivated throughout your study sessions.

Example: Completing Administrative Tasks
Administrative activities, such as filing papers or reacting to emails, may build up and contribute to procrastination. To solve this, set up separate periods for each activity type. For instance, designate 30 minutes to file papers, another 20 minutes to react to emails, and so on. Breaking

down these chores into concentrated sessions helps you keep organized and avoids them from getting overwhelming.

Example: Starting a Personal Project
Launching a personal endeavor, like establishing a blog or learning a new skill, may be tough without a clear strategy. Break the project into segments and manageable milestones. For instance, schedule one week to research, another to build an outline, and the following weeks to finish various parts. Celebrate each milestone attained, as it puts you closer to fulfilling your project objectives.

Developing Effective Study and Work Habits

Example: Establishing a Consistent Study Routine Consistency is crucial to excellent study habits. Choose a fixed time and location to study regularly, preferably free from distractions. For example, designate 7-9 PM each evening as your study hour and construct a separate study location. By making this a habit, your mind will automatically change into "study mode" during certain hours, leading to enhanced productivity.

Example: Implementing the "Two-Minute Rule" at Work

To do lesser jobs effectively, utilize the "Two-Minute Rule." If a job takes less than two minutes to accomplish, do it promptly. For instance, if you get an email that demands a concise answer, react straight away. By adopting this behavior, you'll avoid trivial activities from stacking up and disturbing your productivity.

Example: Setting Priorities using the "Eisenhower Matrix"

Use the Eisenhower Matrix to prioritize activities based on their urgency and significance. Identify high-priority and time-sensitive activities and handle them first. For instance, if you have a project deadline coming, concentrate on it before other less essential chores. By arranging your priorities, you'll devote your time and energy more efficiently.

Example: Utilizing a Focus Timer for Work Sessions

Implement the "focus timer" strategy to sustain productivity throughout work sessions. Set a timer for a set timeframe, say 45 minutes, and commit to working on a single job with undivided concentration until the timer goes off. After the session, take a brief rest before commencing the next concentrated work session. This strategy improves your work while offering occasional downtime for brain refreshment.

Example: Creating a Weekly Planner for Work Projects

Use a weekly calendar to set out your professional activities and responsibilities. Write down deadlines, meetings, and particular project milestones. Allocate allocated periods for each work and adhere to your timetable. This habit allows you to manage your time properly, ensuring that no jobs are overlooked or left to the last minute.

Strategies for Staying Motivated and Overcoming Setbacks

Example: Celebrating Small Achievements
Recognize and appreciate even the tiniest victories. Completing a task, accomplishing a milestone, or getting great comments from a coworker are all worth celebrating. Treat yourself to a favorite snack or take a brief pause to acknowledge your accomplishment. These modest incentives enhance motivation and reinforce beneficial behavior.

Example: Utilizing Visualization Techniques
Visualize your objectives and achievement consistently. Picture yourself accomplishing activities, presenting a successful presentation, or obtaining your desired objectives. Visualization may enhance drive and confidence, making setbacks seem transient and surmountable.

Example: Seeking Support from a Mentor or Coach

Having a mentor or coach may give significant insight and encouragement. When confronting setbacks or uncertainty, turn to your mentor for guidance and support. They may give insights based on their experiences, helping you negotiate obstacles with more resilience.

Example: Setting Realistic Goals and Deadlines
Establish feasible objectives and realistic dates for your tasks. Overcommitting oneself may lead to fatigue and dissatisfaction. Set reasonable targets and divide bigger activities into smaller, doable stages. Accomplishing these objectives within acceptable periods provides a feeling of success and drive.

Example: Learning from Setbacks and Adapting
Embrace setbacks as learning opportunities rather than failures. When a task doesn't go as planned, reflect on what went wrong and find opportunities for improvement. Use these lessons to alter your strategy and develop your methods for future initiatives. A growth

mentality permits failures to become stepping stones toward achievement.

By reducing things into manageable pieces, adopting good study and work routines, and applying tactics for remaining motivated and overcoming setbacks, you may greatly enhance your productivity. Remember that productivity is a path of continual growth, and with commitment and effort, you can reach your objectives and maximize your potential.

Chapter 7: Developing Effective Retention Strategies

As someone with ADHD, you may have faced difficulty with typical study strategies. However, by adapting your approach to meet your particular strengths and limitations, you may optimize your learning experience and boost retention.

Example: Utilizing Visual Aids and Mind Maps
Visual aids, such as diagrams, charts, and mind maps, are important tools for arranging information in a manner that corresponds with ADHD cognitive processes. When learning complicated subjects, construct colorful mind maps that link related ideas. These visual representations may help you comprehend and remember knowledge more efficiently.

Example: Incorporating Movement and Kinesthetic Learning
ADHD people typically benefit from learning via movement and physical involvement. When

studying, consider introducing kinesthetic components into your routine. For instance, move about while studying flashcards, or use hand gestures to highlight crucial points during a lecture. Associating movement with learning helps enhance concentration and memory retention.

Example: Using Mnemonic Devices
Mnemonic devices are memory aids that help you recall information via associations. Create interesting and unique mnemonics to recall crucial information or lists. For example, to recall the sequence of the planets, you may use the phrase "My Very Educated Mother Just Served Us Noodles," where each word corresponds to a planet in the solar system.

Memory Enhancement Techniques

Enhancing memory is vital for effective learning. Incorporate these memory improvement tactics into your study regimen to boost knowledge retention.

Example: Spaced Repetition
Spaced repetition entails revisiting knowledge at increasingly increasing intervals. When studying, review topics at defined intervals, such as after one day, one week, and one month. This strategy enhances long-term memory, making it simpler to remember knowledge when required.

Example: Practicing Retrieval
Actively retrieve material from memory during study sessions. Instead of passively perusing notes, cover them up and seek to recollect crucial ideas or information. This activity develops memory pathways and enhances your capacity to retain knowledge for tests or presentations.

Example: Making Personal Connections
Relate new material to your own experiences or previous knowledge. When learning a new subject, ask yourself how it connects to real-life situations or topics you already understand.

Creating these links boosts memory retention and enriches your grasp of the topic.

Improving Reading Comprehension and Information Retention

Effective reading comprehension is vital for acquiring and remembering knowledge. Incorporate these tactics into your reading regimen to boost comprehension and retention.

Example: Active Reading with Annotations
Engage actively while reading by scribbling comments and notes in the margins or using sticky notes. Highlight noteworthy points, ask questions, or write down links to other subjects. This interactive technique helps you remain focused and recall vital knowledge.

Example: Summarizing and Paraphrasing
After reading a section or chapter, describe the important ideas in your own words. Paraphrasing helps strengthen your knowledge of the content and promotes retention. Practice summarizing

complicated topics until you can convey them simply and succinctly.

Example: Discussing with Peers
Engage in conversations with classmates, friends, or study groups about the content you've read. Talking and discussing the subject helps you to explain your knowledge and hear alternative viewpoints, boosting your comprehension and retention.

By adapting study tactics to fit your ADHD strengths, using memory enhancement techniques, and boosting reading comprehension skills, you may establish successful retention strategies. These individualized ways will help you to overcome learning problems, remember knowledge more effectively, and achieve in your academic endeavors and beyond. enjoy your learning style, try these tactics, and enjoy the thrill of constant learning and improvement.

Chapter 8: Navigating Work and Career with ADHD

Deciding whether to reveal your ADHD to employers and coworkers may be a tough issue. Let's investigate real-life examples to assist you through this process.

Example: Disclosing ADHD to a Supportive Employer

You've been working at a firm for a few months, and you feel comfortable with your boss and coworkers. You find that your ADHD symptoms sometimes impair your job performance. After considerable contemplation, you decide to report your ADHD to your boss. To your relief, your company is sympathetic and responsive, giving assistance and appropriate modifications to help you excel in your position. This transparency generates a healthy and supportive work atmosphere, helping you to overcome problems with more ease.

Example: Choosing Not to Disclose ADHD Initially

You start a new job and decide not to reveal your ADHD straight immediately. You like to examine the work environment and create a feeling of trust with your colleagues before providing this personal information. Over time, you recognize that you may benefit from certain adjustments. Eventually, you reveal your ADHD to your boss, who proves to be sympathetic and helpful, exactly as you had anticipated. Your choice to wait until you were comfortable and secure in your employment paid off and you now have the necessary support to excel in your career.

Strategies for Managing Work Responsibilities and Deadlines

Effectively managing job duties and deadlines is crucial for professional success. Let's review techniques to assist you keep on top of your work.

Example: Using Task Management Apps
You find it tough to recall all your job projects and deadlines, so you start using a task management tool like Todoist or Trello. You enter your assignments, set due dates, and get reminders to keep you on track. The program helps you prioritize work, manage time wisely, and finish projects on schedule, minimizing the stress of managing various commitments.

Example: Breaking Projects into Milestones
You're handed a major assignment with a tight deadline. Rather than feeling overwhelmed, you split the endeavor into tiny stages. Each milestone becomes a new item on your to-do list. This strategy enables you to concentrate on one component at a time, making the job more manageable and assuring consistent progress toward completion.

Creating a Work Environment Conducive to Productivity

A supportive work environment may substantially improve your productivity and job happiness. Consider these ways to establish a workplace that boosts your attention and efficiency.

Example: Minimizing Distractions
You detect typical irritants in your office, such as boisterous colleagues or messy surroundings. To reduce distractions, you invest in noise-canceling headphones to shut out annoying noises. Additionally, you declutter your workplace, keeping just important objects within reach. These adjustments promote a more focused and favorable work atmosphere.

Example: Advocating for Flexible Work Arrangements
You find that your ADHD symptoms tend to be more tolerable during specific hours of the day. You discuss this with your boss and offer a flexible work arrangement. With their agreement, you alter your calendar to match

your peak production hours, leading to increased performance and a healthier work-life balance.

Navigating a job and career with ADHD demands a careful and proactive strategy. Whether you choose to reveal your ADHD or manage it secretly, employing tactics for task management, establishing a favorable work environment, and asking for appropriate accommodations will empower you to prosper in your career. Embrace your unique abilities, harness available resources, and prioritize your well-being to navigate the working world with confidence and success.

Chapter 9: Managing Emotional Well-being and Stress

Living with ADHD may bring about a variety of feelings, and knowing its emotional effect is a critical step in managing your well-being. Let's review the emotions typically connected with ADHD and the techniques to handle them.

Example: Frustration with Inattention and Forgetfulness
You regularly find yourself annoyed by bouts of inattention and forgetfulness, such as misplacing your possessions or forgetting essential aspects in talks. Recognize that these obstacles are a component of ADHD and not a reflection of your ability. By realizing this, you may cultivate patience and self-compassion, treating yourself with love when confronted with these situations.

Example: Impatience with Hyperactivity and Restlessness

Your hyperactivity and restlessness may sometimes lead to irritation with yourself or others. Instead of considering these attributes as hindrances, examine the wonderful features they contribute, such as endless energy and passion. Embrace your high energy as a unique quality and channel it into activities that provide pleasure and delight.

Coping Mechanisms for Stress and Overwhelm

Stress and overload are frequent sensations for those with ADHD. Adopting coping techniques may help you handle stressful circumstances and build emotional resilience.

Example: Taking Breaks to Regain Focus
When feeling overwhelmed by various jobs or duties, take small pauses to regroup and refuel. Step away from your job or the scenario creating tension, and participate in a relaxing activity like deep breathing or a brief stroll. These periods of relaxation might help cleanse your thoughts and

boost attention when you return to the activity at hand.

Example: Journaling to Express Emotions
Consider maintaining a diary to communicate your ideas and feelings. Writing about your experiences and feelings may serve as a therapeutic outlet, helping you achieve clarity and manage emotions. By admitting and facing emotions, you make room for healing and development.

Cultivating Mindfulness and Self-Care Practices

Practicing mindfulness and self-care may dramatically affect your emotional well-being. Here are techniques to nurture these behaviors in your everyday life.

Example: Mindful Breathing to Reduce Stress
When feeling overwhelmed or nervous, try mindful breathing. Take a few minutes to concentrate entirely on your breath, inhaling and expelling deeply. Mindful breathing may

stimulate the body's relaxation response, lowering tension and generating a sensation of peace.

Example: Engaging in Activities that Bring Joy Make time for hobbies that offer you delight and pleasure. Whether it's following a hobby, spending time with loved ones, or immersing yourself in nature, participating in activities that feed your soul may increase your emotional well-being and resilience.

In conclusion, managing emotional well-being and stress with ADHD entails recognizing the emotional effect of the disease, developing coping strategies for stress and overload, and fostering mindfulness and self-care practices. By accepting your unique qualities, practicing self-compassion, and prioritizing emotional health, you may traverse the obstacles of ADHD with more ease and cultivate a pleasant and rewarding emotional environment.

Remember that it's necessary to seek professional assistance if feelings become overpowering, and know that you are capable of creating a solid foundation of emotional well-being and resilience.

Chapter 10: Building Healthy Habits and Lifestyle Choices

Incorporating regular exercise and physical activity into your lifestyle may have a tremendous influence on treating ADHD symptoms and general well-being. Let's discuss why exercise is vital and how you may fit it into your everyday routine.

Example: Boosting Focus and Attention
You notice that on days when you participate in physical exercise, your ability to concentrate and maintain attention increases dramatically. Exercise boosts blood flow to the brain, encouraging the release of neurotransmitters that promote cognitive performance. Whether it's a brisk stroll, a bike ride, or a training session, physical exercise may sharpen your mind and help with your everyday responsibilities.

Example: Reducing Hyperactivity and Restlessness

Regular exercise may help channel surplus energy and lessen symptoms of restlessness. Engaging in physical activities enables you to release pent-up energy in a constructive and useful way, leading to a calmer and more balanced state of mind.

Nutrition Tips for Managing ADHD Symptoms

Nutrition has a crucial role in sustaining brain health and treating ADHD symptoms. Let's investigate dietary ideas to boost your well-being.

Example: Balancing Protein and Carbohydrates
Maintaining a balanced diet with an optimum mix of protein to carbs will help regulate blood sugar levels. Fluctuations in blood sugar might affect mood and attentiveness. Incorporate lean proteins, healthy grains, and fresh fruits and vegetables into your meals to sustain stable energy levels throughout the day.

Example: Omega-3 Fatty Acids for Brain Health

Include foods high in omega-3 fatty acids, such as fatty fish (salmon, mackerel, sardines) and flaxseeds, in your diet. Omega-3 fatty acids are vital for brain health, maintaining good cognitive function and emotional well-being.

Developing Healthy Sleep Routines

Quality sleep is crucial for cognitive performance and emotional stability. Cultivating proper sleep patterns may greatly improve your entire well-being.

Example: Establishing a Consistent Sleep Schedule
Try to keep a regular sleep routine, especially on weekends. Going to bed and getting up at the same time each day helps regulate your body's internal clock and enhances the quality of your sleep.

Example: Creating a Relaxing Bedtime Routine
Develop a relaxing sleep ritual to inform your body that it's time to shut down. Engage in

activities that encourage relaxation, such as reading a book, doing mild stretches, or meditating. Limit screen time before bed, since exposure to blue light might alter sleep patterns.

In conclusion, adopting healthy behaviors and lifestyle choices is vital for treating ADHD symptoms and increasing overall well-being. Regular exercise promotes attention and lowers restlessness, while a healthy diet supports cognitive performance and emotional stability.

Prioritizing quality sleep develops good brain health and emotional stability. Embrace these lifestyle choices and apply them to your daily routine to develop a healthier, happier, and more meaningful life with ADHD. Remember that tiny, regular actions lead to substantial improvements, and you can build a lifestyle that enables you to flourish.

Chapter 11: Strategies for Effective Communication and Relationships

Effective communication is the cornerstone of strong partnerships. Let's examine techniques to increase your communication abilities and establish meaningful relationships with others.

Example: Active Listening
Practice active listening by giving your complete attention to the speaker. Maintain eye contact, nod to express comprehension, and avoid interrupting. Reflect on what the individual is saying before answering. Active listening creates trust and empathy, establishing a solid basis for open and honest conversation.

Example: Using "I" Statements
When expressing your views or worries, utilize "I" statements instead of "you" phrases. For instance, say, "I feel overwhelmed when there's too much noise around me," instead of "You

always make too much noise!" "I" comments prevent blame and enable a more productive and understanding discourse.

Managing Impulsivity and Emotional Regulation in Relationships

ADHD may often contribute to impulsive behaviors and emotional intensity in relationships. Here are techniques to control impulsivity and promote emotional regulation.

Example: Pause and Breathe
When presented with a circumstance that causes impulsive or high emotions, take a minute to stop and take deep breaths. Giving yourself this space helps you to gather your thoughts and reply in a calmer and more considerate way.

Example: Practice Mindfulness
Incorporate mindfulness practices into your routine to improve emotional awareness. Mindfulness helps you identify and appreciate your emotions without judgment, helping you to

behave more logically and empathetically in stressful circumstances.

Nurturing Supportive and Understanding Connections

Building supportive and understanding connections is vital for your emotional well-being. Here are techniques to develop such ties.

Example: Be Open About ADHD Challenges
Share your experiences with ADHD with trustworthy friends and loved ones. Being transparent about your struggles and talents encourages empathy and support. True friends and loving partners will appreciate your honesty and give support and aid when required.

Example: Set Boundaries and Communicate Needs
Establish clear boundaries and explain your demands within your relationships. Let people know when you need some space or when

certain habits are overbearing. Setting boundaries ensures that your emotional well-being is emphasized, and it creates reciprocal respect in your relationships.

In conclusion, efficient communication and healthy relationships are vital for your mental health and general well-being. By practicing active listening, employing "I" statements, and limiting impulsivity, you may develop greater relationships with people. Mindfulness and emotional control practices equip you to behave wisely and empathetically in stressful circumstances.

Openness about your ADHD issues, coupled with establishing limits and expressing needs, develops supportive and understanding relationships with individuals who genuinely appreciate and care for you. Embrace these tactics and engage in developing meaningful connections that enhance your life and contribute to your personal development and satisfaction.

Chapter 12: Thriving in Academic Settings: Strategies for Students with ADHD

As a student with ADHD, asking for accommodations in your academic setting is vital to support your learning and academic achievement. Let's discuss techniques to successfully advocate for your needs.

Example: Requesting Extended Test Time
You find that you struggle to finish tests within the regular time range owing to your ADHD-related issues. After researching potential accommodations, you visit your school's disability services office to seek longer test times.

By presenting appropriate documents and outlining how this accommodation will help you show your knowledge without the pressure of time restrictions, you effectively acquire the assistance you need to perform your best on tests.

Example: Using a Quiet Testing Environment
You notice that noise and distractions greatly impair your concentration during examinations. To solve this difficulty, you engage with your instructors and seek a quiet testing setting as an accommodation. You explain how a peaceful situation will help you to focus better and operate at your maximum capacity.

With understanding faculty assistance, you are provided a separate room for tests, establishing an atmosphere favorable to your performance.

Building Resilience and Overcoming Academic Challenges

Overcoming academic problems is feasible with resilience and smart tactics. Let's examine approaches to develop resilience and prosper in your academic career.

Example: Breaking Tasks into Manageable Steps
You typically struggle with arranging and finishing long-term projects. To address this, you

start breaking down activities into smaller, more manageable pieces. For a research paper, you establish timelines for picking a subject, doing research, outlining, writing drafts, and rewriting. By concentrating on one step at a time, you create momentum and effectively finish the job.

Example: Utilizing Time Management Techniques
You frequently find yourself swamped by various tasks and deadlines. To manage your time more successfully, you embrace the Pomodoro Technique, setting a timer for intense work times followed by brief breaks. By designating defined time blocks for each task, you improve productivity, retain concentration, and decrease stress.

Seeking Support and Resources

In addition to lobbying for accommodations, finding assistance and using accessible resources will further improve your academic experience.

Example: Joining Study Groups
Recognizing the advantages of collaborative learning, you join a study group with individuals who share your academic interests. Working together, you discuss ideas, study course content, and give each other support and encouragement. This study group becomes a vital resource, helping you comprehend topics and perform better in your classes.

Example: Utilizing Academic Support Services
Your institution provides academic assistance programs, including tutoring and study skills courses. Recognizing the need for further support, you attend tutoring sessions on topics you find tough. Through individualized teaching and assistance, you get a better comprehension of the content and enhance your academic achievement.

In conclusion, succeeding in academic settings as a student with ADHD entails successfully advocating for accommodations, establishing resilience to overcome hurdles, and using available support and resources. By pushing for accommodations, you create an inclusive learning environment that meets your specific needs. Building resilience and executing effective techniques allow you to face academic hurdles with confidence and success. Seeking help from classmates, study groups, and academic services increases your learning experience and adds to your overall development and academic success. Embrace these tactics, make the most of available resources, and take pleasure in your path as a resilient and successful student with ADHD.

Chapter 13: Financial Management and Organization

Budgeting is a vital component of financial management, especially for those with ADHD who may experience issues with impulsivity and organization. Let's discuss practical budgeting ideas to help you take control of your money.

Example: The Envelope System
You struggle to keep track of your spending and frequently find yourself surpassing your budget on discretionary things. To remedy this, you employ the envelope system. At the beginning of each month, you designate funds for certain expenditure categories, such as grocery, entertainment, and transportation. You deposit the cash in labeled envelopes and utilize just the authorized amount for each category. This concrete technique helps you physically comprehend your spending boundaries and minimizes excess.

Example: Utilizing Budgeting Apps

Managing funds using conventional techniques may be stressful. Instead, you select a budgeting program like Mint or YNAB (You Need a Budget). These applications integrate with your accounts, classify costs, and give visual reports on your spending patterns. The app's alerts and reminders help you remain accountable to your budgeting objectives, creating a better awareness of your financial status.

Overcoming Impulsive Spending Habits

ADHD impulsivity may lead to impulsive spending, making it tough to stay within a budget. Here are techniques to limit impulsive spending and encourage better financial decision-making.

Example: Implementing a "30-Day Rule"
When tempted to make impulsive purchases, you apply a "30-day rule." Instead of purchasing the item immediately, you wait for 30 days before making a choice. During this period, you analyze whether the purchase corresponds with your

requirements and financial objectives. Often, the waiting time lets you recognize that the urge was ephemeral, protecting you from unpleasant impulsive purchases.

Example: Creating a Spending Plan

You know that impulsive spending generally happens when you don't have a clear strategy for your money. To fight this, you prepare a thorough spending plan at the beginning of each month. This plan contains your critical costs, savings objectives, and discretionary spending restrictions. Having a planned strategy helps you to make thoughtful spending decisions and reduces impulsive purchases.

Organizing Financial Documents and Paperwork

Maintaining structured financial papers and documentation is vital for monitoring costs and staying on top of your financial health. Let's study techniques to enhance financial organization.

Example: Utilizing Digital Document Storage
You struggle with paper clutter and regularly lose essential financial paperwork. To simplify organizing, you digitize your financial documentation using tools like Evernote or Google Drive. You create folders to organize documents, such as bills, receipts, and tax-related files. This digital method offers instant access to essential information and avoids the burden of physical paper maintenance.

Example: Setting Up a Financial Calendar
To keep on track with bill payments and financial duties, you construct a financial calendar. You designate due dates for bills, subscription renewals, and other financial responsibilities. Additionally, you set reminders on your phone to inform you a few days before the due dates. This proactive strategy guarantees you never miss a payment and develops improved financial management.

In conclusion, efficient financial management and organization for people with ADHD entail budgeting tactics, controlling impulsive spending patterns, and arranging financial data. By adopting the envelope method or utilizing budgeting applications, you get more control over your resources and expenditures. Implementing the "30-Day Rule" and making a spending plan help you make conscious financial choices and minimize impulsiveness. Embracing digital document storage and putting up a financial calendar improves financial management and keeps you on top of critical deadlines and obligations. With these techniques in place, you may attain more financial stability and peace of mind, helping you to succeed in your financial journey with ADHD.

Chapter 14: Embracing Neurodiversity: Harnessing the Strengths of ADHD

ADHD carries with it a variety of abilities that may be used to attain success and personal satisfaction. Let's explore and cherish these distinct qualities.

Example: Hyperfocus and Intense Concentration
You've encountered times of hyperfocus when you get fully immersed in an activity that captivates your attention. This degree of focus helps you to accomplish exceptional productivity and creativity. Embracing this capability, you learn to discover things that cause hyperfocus and deliberately integrate them into your career and pastimes.

Example: Resilience and Adaptability
Living with ADHD has taught you to adapt and navigate through many hurdles. This resilience

develops a development attitude, helping you to confront problems with drive and tenacity. Embracing your versatility, you discover new solutions to issues, making you a valued asset in changing circumstances.

Leveraging Creativity and Innovation

ADHD typically goes hand in hand with a natural tendency towards creativity and invention. Embrace these attributes to enhance personal and professional progress.

Example: Embracing "Out-of-the-Box" Thinking Your mind is good at generating unique connections between apparently unrelated topics. You employ this expertise to provide new insights and unique solutions to projects and debates. Embracing your "out-of-the-box" thinking, you contribute to innovative brainstorming sessions and urge others to explore new routes.

Example: Embracing Divergent Thinking

Divergent thinking, a characteristic of ADHD, permits you to produce several ideas and solutions for a given difficulty. Embracing this technique, you explore many alternatives without self-censorship. This flexibility brings up new chances for problem-solving and creates a culture of innovation in your personal and professional life.

Celebrating Neurodiversity and Challenging Stigmas

Neurodiversity is a basic component of the human experience, and embracing it challenges stigmas connected with ADHD. Let's discuss the relevance of honoring neurodiversity.

Example: Fostering Inclusive Environments
In educational and corporate contexts, you push for inclusiveness and appreciate neurodiversity. By fostering knowledge and acceptance of varied learning and working methods, you help to establish an atmosphere where all people may

succeed, regardless of their neurodivergent qualities.

Example: Redefining Success on Your Terms
You disrupt society's conventions and expectations by redefining success on your terms. Instead of judging success purely by standard measurements, you prioritize personal progress, pleasure, and contentment. Embracing your unique abilities and viewpoint, you encourage others to accept their neurodiversity and boldly follow their interests.

In conclusion, embracing neurodiversity and utilizing the qualities of ADHD is a profound path of self-discovery and personal progress. Recognizing your particular qualities, such as hyperfocus and perseverance, helps you to harness these characteristics to achieve amazing achievements. Embracing creativity and diverse thinking helps you to develop and provide new views to different facets of life. By celebrating neurodiversity and combating stigmas, you contribute to establishing inclusive cultures that recognize varied abilities and viewpoints. Embrace your neurodivergent identity, celebrate your abilities, and encourage others to recognize the beauty of neurodiversity in all its manifestations.

Chapter 15: Maintaining Long-Term Success and Growth

Maintaining long-term success and development entails defining relevant objectives and adopting tactics to attain them. Let's investigate how you may establish and pursue your objectives efficiently.

Example: Setting S.M.A.R.T. Goals
You've learned the benefits of creating Specific, Measurable, Achievable, Relevant, and Time-bound (S.M.A.R.T.) objectives. Instead of abstract goals, you set precise and achievable objectives. For instance, you create a goal to finish a certification program within six months, describing the procedures necessary to attain it. This method keeps you engaged and motivated, making long-term success more realistic.

Example: Breaking Down Goals into Milestones

You realize that long-term objectives might seem daunting without breaking them down into smaller stages. By separating your objectives into manageable segments, you build a blueprint for achievement. For instance, if your long-term aim is to create a company, you break it down into activities like performing market research, drafting a business plan, and building a website. Celebrating each milestone's accomplishment builds your confidence and continues momentum towards long-term achievement.

Developing Resilience and Adaptability

Resilience and flexibility are crucial traits in sustaining long-term success despite obstacles and changes. Let's investigate how you can nurture these traits.

Example: Learning from Setbacks
You've met difficulties on your road, but you view them as chances for improvement. Rather than feeling disheartened, you examine the scenario, discover lessons learned, and apply

them to future initiatives. This resilient mindset helps you to bounce back stronger and wiser from life's adversities.

Example: Embracing Change as an Opportunity
You know that life is dynamic, and adaptation is crucial for long-term progress. Embracing change as an opportunity rather than a threat helps you to pivot when required and welcome new opportunities. For example, while encountering adjustments in your employment or personal life, you perceive them as opportunities for personal and professional development, leading to continuing progress beyond your ADHD journey.

Continuing Personal and Professional Growth Beyond ADHD

Maintaining long-term success needs constant personal and professional improvement. Let's discuss how you may embrace lifelong learning and growth.

Example: Pursuing Continuing Education
You appreciate information and skills growth, so you actively seek out possibilities for continuous education. Whether it's taking online courses, attending seminars, or seeking further degrees, you embrace lifelong learning to remain current and competitive in your profession.

Example: Engaging in Networking and Mentorship
You realize the benefits of networking and mentoring in your personal and professional progress. You actively engage in business events, join professional groups, and seek help from experienced mentors. These relationships enrich your ideas and give important assistance in your quest for long-term success.

In conclusion, sustaining long-term success and progress entails creating S.M.A.R.T. objectives, breaking them down into milestones, and fostering resilience and flexibility. Embracing failures as chances for learning and perceiving change positively supports continuing growth.

By embracing lifelong learning, participating in networking, and seeking mentoring, you lay the road for continued personal and professional progress beyond your ADHD experience. Remember that long-term success is a path of ongoing self-improvement, and with determination, perseverance, and an open mind, you can continue to flourish and achieve excellence in all parts of life.

Conclusion: Embracing the Power of ADHD: Your Journey to Success

Throughout this book, we have explored the tactics and insights to help you embrace the potential of ADHD and go on a road of achievement and personal development. As we complete this transformational inquiry, let's examine the important insights from each chapter and give encouragement for the path ahead.

In Chapter 1, "Understanding ADHD: An Overview of Attention Deficit Hyperactivity Disorder," we explored the symptoms and issues associated with ADHD. We discovered that ADHD is not a restriction but a distinct way of viewing the world. By acknowledging and comprehending our particular experiences, we get the strength to grow beyond any limits.

Chapter 2, "The Power of Self-Awareness: Embracing Your ADHD," underlined the necessity of identifying and embracing our ADHD diagnosis. We addressed our strengths and shortcomings, learning to use our strong traits while adopting self-compassion and a positive approach toward our situation. This self-awareness permits us to build a path of honesty and personal satisfaction.

In Chapter 3, "Building an Effective Support System," we recognized the value of our support network. We learned to depend on family, friends, therapists, coaches, mentors, and support groups. These relationships give empathy, encouragement, and useful insights, confirming our capacity to manage obstacles with confidence.

Chapter 4, "Time Management and Organization Strategies," presented us with methods to develop successful routines, prioritize activities, and employ time management applications. These tactics assist us to optimize productivity and avoid stress, allowing us to flourish in our activities.

In Chapter 5, "Overcoming Procrastination and Enhancing Focus," we discussed typical reasons for procrastination and investigated approaches like the Pomodoro Technique and time blocking. Armed with these approaches, we may beat procrastination and strengthen our attention, unleashing our full potential.

Chapter 6, "Boosting Productivity: Strategies for Getting Things Done," taught us to split activities into manageable parts, build study and work routines, and remain motivated despite failures. With these methods, we keep continuous momentum toward our objectives.

In Chapter 7, "Developing Effective Retention Strategies," we customized our study approaches to meet our ADHD strengths and limitations. We examined memory improvement approaches and refined our reading comprehension and knowledge retention abilities, boosting our learning capacity.

Chapter 8, "Navigating Work and Career with ADHD," helped us in revealing ADHD to employers and coworkers and managing our job obligations and deadlines. By building a suitable work atmosphere, we may flourish in our vocations with honesty and confidence.

In Chapter 9, "Managing Emotional Well-being and Stress," we learned to manage the emotional effect of ADHD, deal with stress and overload, and emphasize mindfulness and self-care activities. These skills promote emotional resilience, paving the road for a healthy and satisfied existence.

Chapter 10, "Building Healthy Habits and Lifestyle Choices," stressed the need for exercise, diet, and appropriate sleep habits. By adopting these behaviors, we boost our well-being and support our success path.

In Chapter 11, "Strategies for Effective Communication and Relationships," we polished our communication skills, regulated impulsivity, and recognized neurodiversity. These tactics establish meaningful connections, developing relationships that strengthen us.

Chapter 12, "Thriving in Academic Settings: Strategies for Students with ADHD," empowered us to argue for adjustments, develop resilience, and overcome stigmas. With these instruments, we embrace academic accomplishment with unrelenting dedication.

Chapter 13, "Financial Management and Organization," enabled us to budget properly, stop impulsive spending habits, and arrange our financial papers. By learning these abilities, we take control of our financial health and security.

In Chapter 14, "Embracing Neurodiversity: Harnessing the Strengths of ADHD," we acknowledged our unique abilities, utilized creativity and innovation, and embraced neurodiversity. Armed with this information, we redefine success on our terms, opening the route for personal and professional advancement.

Finally, in Chapter 15, "Maintaining Long-Term Success and Growth," we strategized long-term goal planning, established resilience and adaptation, and welcomed continuing personal and professional improvement. Armed with persistence and an open mind, we continue to grow and accomplish greatness beyond our ADHD path.

As you go on your adventure, remember that you are not alone. Embrace your ADHD and your particular skills, because they are the keys to unlocking your entire potential. Celebrate every milestone, learn from failures, and accept change with unrelenting drive. Your road will have its hurdles, but with resilience, support, and the skills gained here, you are bound for greatness.

Remember, this is just the beginning. There are innumerable tools and references accessible to further study and expand your knowledge of ADHD. Seek information, network with like-minded folks, and continue to develop and change on your route to success.

Believe in yourself, accept your path, and appreciate the strength of ADHD inside you. The world is waiting for your talent, and with sincerity, tenacity, and unrelenting resolve, you will succeed beyond your wildest dreams. Go out, and may your journey be blessed with prosperity, pleasure, and satisfaction. Your adventure has just started, and the possibilities are unlimited. Embrace the power of ADHD, and embrace the strength inside you.